Revealing Love

Pray Now
Daily Devotions
Monthly Prayers
and How to Pray

Published on behalf of the
PRAY NOW GROUP

SAINT ANDREW PRESS
Edinburgh

First published in 2013 by
SAINT ANDREW PRESS
121 George Street
Edinburgh EH2 4YN

Copyright © Pray Now Group, Faith Expressions Team, Mission and
Discipleship Council, The Church of Scotland 2014

ISBN 978 0 86153 805 8

British Library Cataloguing in Publication Data
A catalogue record for this book is available from the British Library.

It is the publisher's policy to only use papers that are natural and
recyclable and that have been manufactured from timber grown in
renewable, properly managed forests. All of the manufacturing processes
of the papers are expected to conform to the environmental regulations of
the country of origin.

Typeset by Waverley Typesetters, Norfolk
Printed and bound in the United Kingdom by
CPI Group (UK) Ltd, Croydon CR0 4YY

Contents

Twelve Additional Monthly Prayers

Preface

We thank You for giving us
enough glimpses of love to cling to,
for answering our complexity
with Your simplicity

Prayer on Day 22

This is a beautiful book. It offers some of the most heart-felt poetry and profound image that invites each of us to explore and lose ourselves in prayer basing our journey on the many images of love found in 1 Corinthians 13. 'Love' is a word that holds so many journeys for us yet it is more than a word: it is the very incarnation of God and the meditations, prayers and blessings in this book open our souls and our faith to incarnation all around us.

God is not always found in the most obvious places and these prayers lift the corners of life enough to reveal a glimpse, an echo, a trysting place of Jesus as we take each day and offer it to God's blessing. Perhaps it will be just a word in the right place, a phrase that leaps from the page, an image that fills a hole but, in each and every way we are drawn into God, it is always a place of love. So be blessed as you use this book in all its simple poetry and invitation to love ourselves, each other and mostly God, that we might echo the prayer on Day 29:

Then side by side,
hand in hand and heart to heart,
in the meeting tent of Your world
may we see ourselves
face to face with Your reflection.

REVD RODDY HAMILTON
Vice-Convener, Faith Expression

Using this Book

And now faith, hope, and love abide, these three;
and the greatest of these is love.

1 Corinthians 13:13

'Revealing Love' is the theme for this edition of *Pray Now*.

God's love is revealed to us in the gift of creation, in the gift of life, in the gift of God's self in Jesus Christ, in the gift of the Holy Spirit and in the gift of our own relationships with God and with each other. Love is the expression of God. Where love is: God is revealed.

In His teaching, Jesus gave simple commandments relating to love. He reaffirmed the first great commandment written in the Hebrew Scriptures to love God with all our being and to love our neighbour. To this He added:

Love one another. Just as I have loved you,
you should also love one another.
By this will everyone know that you are my disciples,
if you have love one for another.

John 13:34–35

Loving one another as Jesus loves us is the distinguishing mark of discipleship.

The *Pray Now* Group chose to base 'Revealing Love' on the popular chapter about love from St Paul's first letter to the Corinthian church. We did so for several reasons.

First, this passage has become well known both inside and outside of the Church through its use at local and national weddings, funerals, baptisms and other ceremonies that celebrate life, love and relationship. The inspirational words of 1 Corinthians 13 move people of all ages from all faiths and beliefs because St Paul describes the characteristics of genuine and Christ-like love with language and images that still speak to people today. The passage is as relevant, enlightening and challenging as it was when it was first written to a deeply divided and troubled church in AD 53–57.

Second, we felt that this text gave us an opportunity to explore further each marker of love St Paul identifies by reflecting on how that quality of love is being revealed today.

The first part of the book is for people who are new to prayer and would like some encouragement in how to pray. We hope also that those who have been praying for many years may use this first section to reflect on their current prayer habits and that those who may be experiencing difficulties in praying might try some of the suggestions.

The main part of the book is in the pattern of previous years with 31 days of prayerful stimuli. Each day is titled by a quotation about love from 1 Corinthians 13 which has been the source for the reflecting and writing.

Each day offers the following:

- a biblical verse that has stimulated the content for the day
- a short meditation
- a short prayer
- two suggestions for scriptural reading
- a blessing.

Each day may be taken as a whole or readers may choose to reflect only on the meditation to prompt personal prayer and next month use the suggested prayer for reflection. You may also wish to take 1 Corinthians 4–7 and substitute your own name for 'love' for example 'Jim is patient'. As well as using this exercise for prayer, you might want to concentrate on one quality of love per week and at the end of each day, reflect on how well you practised that quality or experienced it from others.

The third part of the book includes twelve monthly prayers. The content of each prayer is based on a broader aspect of love in terms of a stage in life or a quality of love such as Sacrificial Love. There are also further Scripture readings suggested and reflective prayer activities. The monthly prayers enable *Pray Now* to be used morning and evening.

Prayer is a channel of love where we may experience the presence of God and trust that God discerns all we long to pray about – with or without words. Sometimes it is almost subconscious, but it is also helpful to set aside time for more focused prayers. Many people use *Pray Now* as an aid to their personal devotions, praying in a chosen place at home or work or outside or while travelling.

The material may also be used as a basis for:

- prayer pairs or a prayer group – in a home or church or via a social networking site such as 'Facebook'
- mid-week or shorter acts of worship with the addition of a hymn and perhaps a discussion element (see the Appendix)
- opening devotions at the beginning of a meeting
- meditations may be used also in main acts of worship if they help the congregation to explore or reflect on one of the Bible readings for the day
- discovery or wedding or baptism classes/workshops with individuals, couples and parents as a way of exploring love and relationships
- a summer series on 'Love' emanating from 1 Corinthians 13 could utilise some of the content of this year's *Pray Now*.

In whatever way you choose to use this book, the *Pray Now* Group pray that you will discover even more about the power of love revealed in your own life, the life of others and the world around you.

The twentieth-century poet, Robert Winnett, wrote at the end of his poem, 'Love's Insight':

> *Love is creative. Your love brings to birth*
> *God's image in the earthiest of earth.*

REVD CAROL FORD
Convener of the Pray Now *Group*

How to Pray

The title of *Pray Now* was chosen to reflect that no matter who we are, where we have been, what we are like; everyone can start where they are and begin to pray, now. We do not have to wait for a special teaching, a particular moment or spiritual feelings. We can quite simply begin as we are and take it from there. Talking to God is for everyone.

It has been said that we learn to pray by praying; not by reading about it. That is why *Pray Now* aims to be an aid to prayer, rather than an explanation. That said, speaking with others and listening to their understanding of prayer can help us reflect upon our own experiences. This new section 'How to Pray' is therefore a collection of thoughts and ideas to help us think about prayer, especially if we are new to it, returning to it or simply want to refresh our prayer life.

One helpful approach is to take as little as five minutes in your day to pray. Each minute is spent on one of the words your parents were always trying to get you to say – hello, sorry, thank you, please and goodbye. Longer can be spent at each stage, of course, but if we are new to or returning to prayer then short strolls rather than marathons may be helpful.

'Hello'

When we meet with people we know we would rarely pounce upon them with a list of apologies or requests. Usually, we would take the time to say hello, look at the person, shake hands, offer a drink of something or some food and ask how they are. Similarly, in prayer we might look for ways to say 'hello' to God. This could simply involve being quiet for a short moment, reading something from the Book of Psalms or focusing your attention on your breathing. Prayers written by others (such as this book) can be of great help. Other ways are lighting a candle to welcome Christ the Light, settling into a favourite chair or making a hot drink symbolising a desire to rest with God.

It may be worth remembering that we never have to 'come into God's presence' but that we are always with God. Times of prayer are simply more intentional moments to make ourselves aware of the ever-present love of God; that 'in Him we live and move and have our being' (Acts 17:28).

Each of these 'hellos' remind us that we have started a conversation with someone important to us and will help us to resist the things that might pull our attention away from spending this time with God.

'Sorry'

Saying 'sorry' in prayer may be best thought of not as a grovelling word, but as a healing word. When in our daily lives with others we admit where we have got things wrong and say sorry, relationships can heal and grow. This is also true of our relationship with God. Rather than berating ourselves for our daily misdemeanours, God invites us to draw close and be open about who we truly are. What am I sorry about? What I am ashamed of? Martin Luther said 'The first rule of prayer is: do not lie to God' and this is what we aim for; a growing sense of God's love that helps us to share all that we are with God.

George McLeod said: 'We should never rise from our prayers still wondering if God has forgiven us.' Yet this is often difficult. In such moments, arranging to speak with a trustworthy person who understands something of our journey into prayer can be invaluable in helping us deepen our sense of forgiveness and a healed relationship with God.

'Thank you'

Much prayer is in response to something God has done first. This is especially true in our prayers of thanks. While there may be much we are aware of and grateful for, a quiet pause before we begin can help us avoid long repetitive lists of thanks. Take a moment to look over today or the day before and try to remember moments where something good took place. Though I may have missed them at the time, where can I now see qualities like (from 1 Corinthians 13:4–7) patience, kindness, honesty, joy, protection, trust, hope, perseverance? Were these ways in which God was showing love to me?

Similarly, we can look at the bigger picture of our whole life, noticing things we may have taken for granted: life-changing opportunities, people who have nurtured us, something that helped us overcome a difficulty or struggle. What has been good for me in my life and how do I now wish to show that I am grateful?

After offering our thanks to God, we may also feel moved to thank others when we see them next. This helps us join our prayers with our living, completing the cycle and begins to tune us in to the moments of God's goodness throughout the day.

'Please'

The Bible is full of instances of people asking God to bless and protect themselves or others. Many of these requests can seem selfish and self-serving, overly bold or even petty. They might seem to lack the kind of 'spirituality' which we expect to see in these faith-filled characters. Perhaps though, their quality lies in their honesty. Their requests, unpretentious and very human, hint to us that prayer is primarily a relationship to explore, not a technique to be perfected.

When it comes to asking God for something, we do not need to pretend to be saints. Author C. S. Lewis said: 'Pray what is in you, not what ought to be in you.' This is where we begin and where we might often return to, honestly telling God what we need and asking for it. This relationship does not demand that we are good, but that we are honest, open to the possibility of growing and changing.

A short pause before we begin can be helpful here too. Notice what concerns come to mind and simply talk to God about them. What is worrying me? What has been at the back of my mind? Do I know of someone with a need for comfort or encouragement? This can help us connect with the requests that come from within. In this way we are baring our hearts with honesty to a loving and living God.

'Goodbye'

With one another we usually have a pattern for saying farewell. People might hug, shake hands, nod and smile and perhaps make arrangements to meet again.

Times of prayer can benefit from similar actions and words. While we know that we do not leave God's presence, bringing clear closure to the time that has been set apart helps us avoid prayers that fizzle out or drift into distraction.

It can be helpful to move towards the end of your prayers with a time of quiet, moving from talking to God to listening to God. If a particular thought comes to mind, you might spend this time talking about it, or simply holding it before God.

Each of *Pray Now*'s 31 days ends with a short blessing that can be used to close your time of prayer. Similarly, using the Lord's Prayer is a wonderful way of gathering all your prayers into one, as we say with people around the world and across century's the words of Jesus that celebrate the welcome, forgiveness, grace and goodness of God.

> Our Father in heaven,
> hallowed be Your name.
> Your kingdom come,
> Your will be done
> on earth as in heaven.
> Give us today our daily bread
> and forgive us our sins,
> as we forgive those who sin against us.
> Save us from the time of trials
> and deliver us from evil.
> For the kingdom, the power and the glory are Yours,
> now and forever.   AMEN.

GRAHAM FENDER-ALLISON
Worship Development Worker, Faith Expression
Secretary to the Pray Now *Group*

Days of the Month

NOISY GONGS AND CLANGING CYMBALS

I have not hidden your saving help within my heart,
I have spoken of your faithfulness and your salvation.

~ Psalm 40:10a ~

Meditation

Amazing,
the sea of flowers,
the fleet of gleaming cars,
the throng of guests,
the silks, the gold, the finery,
the glittering rings,
the feast of food on groaning tables,
and yet, an emptiness
in the midst of it all –
and in their eyes.

Astonishing,
the shiny pram,
the exquisite nursery,
the nanny in uniform,
the school: exclusive and expensive,
the designer clothes,
the horse, the holidays, the gifts
and yet, a loneliness
in the midst of it all –
and in their hearts.

Surprising,
the silent advent,
the simple home,
the strong, skilled hands,
the hidden life,
the walking, the gathering, the teaching,
the giving
and, in the midst of it,
the love, the challenge,

the compassion
for us all.

Prayer

Lord,
why do we get it so wrong?
why do we think we need to make a noise,
to draw attention to what we have
when what really matters is what we are?
Noisy gongs and clanging cymbals
get people's backs up.
They disturb and exasperate,
whereas love brings solace and peace.
Forgive us, Lord, when we forget these things,
when we bluster on, all puffed up,
trying to fool others into thinking we love well
yet all the time we're hollow inside.
Help us to love silently, deeply, truly,
as You have loved us.
In Jesus' name we ask.   AMEN.

Suggested Readings

Psalm 40   *Not pride, but quiet confidence*
Matthew 6:1–6   *Jesus teaches us*

Blessing

How silently, how silently
the wondrous gift is given!
Lord, You impart to human hearts
the blessings of Your heaven.
No ear may hear His coming,
but in this world of sin,
where meek souls will receive Him, still
the dear Christ enters in.

PROPHETIC POWERS

We have gifts that differ according to the grace given to us:
prophecy, in proportion to faith …

~ Romans 12:6 ~

Meditation

It's not unusual
to be fascinated by superheroes.
Wouldn't it be amazing
to leap tall towers in a single bound;
to climb high buildings and cast a web
over those who fail to match our expectations;
to step into a telephone box,
or spin spectacularly
and find ourselves dressed
ready for the latest crowd-pleasing
defeat of the baddies?

Biblical prophets could easily be confused
with superheroes,
for they call down fire
to demonstrate the weakness of others;
they miraculously fill empty jars
so that they and others might be fed;
they appear from nowhere
and disappear in clouds;
they offer visions
that unsettle those who hear.

With ordinary human attributes,
God places the gift within
the prophets that He chooses
powerfully to portray His message of love.

Prayer

Pouring Your Spirit into human life,
You, Creating God,
are always at work

as You build the foundations for relationships
that will bring justice and restoration
to the communities in which we live.
You place within the heart of individuals
the treasure of Your grace
that makes them Your prophets
within the time they live.
With Your voice
they speak of Your ambition
for respecting all that surrounds;
with Your touch,
they caress the wounds
of careless words,
with Your passion
they unsettle the easy passage of life
to notice the bereft and bereaved;
the hungry and the homeless;
the weary and the wounded.

Wherever and whenever Your Spirit pours forth,
may there be ears and eyes
that welcome the power
of the gift of prophecy
and inspired by its vision
respond in the knowledge
of Christ's presence.   AMEN.

Readings

Joel 2:28–32   *The day of the Lord*
Romans 12:1–8   *Reflecting God in life*

Blessing

Blessed by God's gift of prophecy,
may You recognise the power
of the vision of His kingdom
told in the stories of Jesus
and stirred in the action of His Spirit
active in the lives of ordinary people.   AMEN.

MYSTERIES

Can you find out the deep things of God?
Can you find out the limit of the Almighty?

~ Job 11:7 ~

Meditation

It is above and beyond ...
the deductive powers of Holmes,
the meticulous observation of Monk,
the intuition of Marple,
the logic of Poirot
and the tenacity of Columbo,
to solve the Mystery that is God.

God baffles the imagination,
confounds human logic
and purveys the elements of
ambiguity and perplexity.

God is 'the riddle
wrapped in mystery
inside an enigma',
that can create something from nothing,
that defines power in terms of service,
that transforms death into new life
and defeats evil with love.

More than we can ever conceive or imagine,
yet present in our very souls.
You are above and beyond ...
yet within and personal.

Such knowledge is indeed
too wonderful for me.

Prayer

Incomparable God,
our minds cannot hold You,

our words cannot express You
and Your goodness and mercy
stretch beyond our capabilities.

And yet out of Your abundant grace
You call us to live our lives
in the brightness of Your presence;
that we may hold each thought and word
to the light of Your truth,
so that we may be truth;
and hold each word and deed
to the light of Your love,
so that we may be love.

Illumine our lives
with Your vivifying presence
that we, in turn, may radiate
your life-giving love to others.   AMEN.

Suggested Readings

Psalm 139   *The inescapable God*
Job 11:7–9   *The deep things of God*

Blessing

You are before me, God, You are behind,
and over me You have spread out your hand;
such knowledge is too wonderful for me,
too high to grasp, too great to understand.   AMEN.

Ian Robertson Pitt-Watson

KNOWLEDGE

*What you have learned and received and heard and seen in me –
practise these things, and the God of peace will be with you.*

~ Philippians 4:9 ~

Meditation

Books gather in my house
they huddle and cuddle in filled shelves
piles grow
stacks accrue.
I love them as I love friends
or memories.
They are me, I say.
My books will tell you all you need to know
of who I am.
Of who I want to be.
A spinal column of other people's thoughts
for me to inhale, to breathe as my own breath,
to understand my world for me,
to fill the gaps in my walls
to stop me having to look out,
as a child from their den,
into the vast oceans outside knowledge
outside facts and ideas and opinions and sure grounded
knowing.
I build a book cave of safety from the storm,
the terrifying storm that threatens
my cosy covers.
The storm that might mean I have to love well,
to love differently,
to love anew.

Prayer

Lord, we fill our lives with exams
with ticks and crosses
with As and Bs
with pass and fail,
but love is ever tested –

there is no knowing it once and then forever,
it must be learned afresh each morning
each second
in each atom and glance.
We can take one knowing to a thousand ends,
O King.
May we take our knowledge,
our achievements and grades,
and may we qualify ourselves to love,
to turn our knowing hands to healing,
to tune our knowing ears to care,
to bend our deep and wondrous sciences
to the ever increasing ocean of need
in our ever-growing, learning world.

Suggested Readings

Philippians 4:4–9	*Rejoicing in the peace of the Lord*
Colossians 1:9–14	*Paul's prayer for God's knowledge*

Blessing

May each fact I learn
each lesson I teach
give me a glimpse
of the incomprehensible love
of the actions and teaching
of Jesus Christ, my Lord
my teacher, Rabboni.

MORTALS AND ANGELS

O come, let us worship and bow down,
Let us kneel before the Lord, our Maker!

~ Psalm 95:6 ~

Meditation

Voices full of charm
make pronouncements
promising the earth,
presenting the heavens,
inviting me to a life
of opulence and ease.

Voices, soft and inviting,
smooth-talk and flatter me;
whispering sweet nothings
in my ears,
holding out the promise
of companionship and joy.

I wish I could trust them,
but strangely
there is no power
in their words.
They do not go deeper
than the surface.
They do not touch me
inside.

Sometimes I wonder:
when He spoke,
could people hear the warmth
of His love?
Could they discern the urgency
of His compassion?
Or could they see these things
in His eyes?

Prayer

Lord God,
sometimes I want to close my ears
to the world around me,
to the voices that fill my head
with unwanted images,
the words that create in me cravings
for things I don't need.
How can I escape
the distractions they provide?
How can I turn away from them
to that which really matters?

Only one thing is needed, Lord.
That's what Jesus said.
Help me to understand His meaning.
Help me to hear clearly His voice
above the din of all the noise
that surrounds me.
And help me to use my voice
to speak with love
in praise and worship of You.
In Jesus' name I pray.   AMEN.

Suggested Readings

Revelation 19:6–9   *Angel voices*
Psalm 95   *Lift your voices in worship*

Blessing

May every voice I hear today
speak to me with love.
May every word I speak today
be filled with love.
May God, who is Love,
be the one thing I seek,
today, tomorrow and forever.   AMEN.

FAITH MOVING MOUNTAINS

… truly I tell you, if you have faith the size of a mustard seed, you will say to this mountain, 'Move from here to there', and it will move; and nothing will be impossible for you.

~ Matthew 17:20 ~

Meditation

Cited on Sinai,
honoured on Horeb,
glorified on Gerizim,
confronted on Carmel,
transfigured on Tabor,
and Ascended on Olives.

It is in such places,
where land meets sky
and Earth caresses Heaven,
places of mist and mystery,
of vistas and visions,
of promises and possibilities;
where Divine communes with humanity.

Yet standing in the foothills of faith,
looking up,
in desire
and fear
and awe,
we soon discover that we too
are already in God's presence
and encircled in God's love.

For God's Spirit is
that light within that shines without,
the divinity in our humanity
that lifts us up
and radiates God's presence
for all to see.

Prayer

Here I am, Lord,
wanting, seeking, asking for more.

Sometimes I feel I don't have enough faith
to move the molehills of my life,
never mind the mountains.

Sometimes I feel I don't have enough love
to give to my family and friends
never mind my enemies.

Sometimes I feel I don't have enough time
to spend with myself
never mind with You.

Confront me with the truths from which
I wrongly turn
and confirm me in the truths by which I rightly live.
Remind me again that You have filled me
with an abundance of faith and love,
to be the person that You know I can be.   AMEN.

Suggested Readings

Psalm 125:1–2   *The security of God's people*
Matthew 17:1–13   *The Transfiguration*

Blessing

May the peace of God surround me,
the grace of God astound me,
the hope of God ground me,
and the love of God abound in me.   AMEN.

I AM NOTHING

In the beginning when God created the heavens and the earth, the earth was a formless void.

~ Genesis 1:1–2a ~

Meditation

It all begins with nothing,
for only then is there space
to fill.
It all begins with nothing,
for only then is there room
to feel.
It all begins with nothing,
for only then can something
break the fall.

Deep down, where nothing moves,
light will find the darkest corner
to ignite and glow and fill the void.
Deep down, where hearts hang empty,
hope will seek the smallest place
to settle and to spread.
Deep down, where souls sigh in defeat,
love will throw a lifeline to a lifetime of grace.

I am nothing, Lord,
but a blank canvas in waiting.
Begin with me.

Prayer

Here I am, Lord,
my pieces tossing and turning,
swirling and shaking
like the universe first stirring.
Without You nothing fits.
You alone shape my meaningless thoughts.
You alone place the missing pieces of my soul.
You alone make me something I am not.

Your love alone is all I need
to find me, to lift me, to fill me.
Love me, Your new creation.   AMEN.

Suggested Readings

Genesis 1:1–4   *The creation*
Psalm 130   *Hope in God*

Blessing

God who fills the universe
whisper your love to me.
God of the galaxies
afford me grace.
God infinite and ultimate
hear my heart of praise.   AMEN.

Twitturgies – Gerard Kelly

GIVING AWAY POSSESSIONS

*No one can serve two masters, for either he will hate the one and
love the other, or he will be devoted to one and despise the other.*

~ Matthew 6:24a ~

Meditation

Some have more than me
some have less
but to think that anyone would be able
to count their possessions
is beyond me.
To list each fork
each shoe
each gadget
each pen,
even my estimations are inventions.
To say I owned:
one bowl
one knife
one change of clothes
one bag
would surely be holiness indeed.

But You say,
no.
That is not enough.
Too little.
Too much.
Freer I would certainly be without the weight of stuff
of things, the fluff collected over years
shored against my ruin.
But still not enough,
but still too much.

Prayer

We look at You with fear, Lord;
Your sleep in boats
Your meals at a dozen dozen tables

the way You walked, the terrifying way You walked
so light on the road, so few things to lose
so much to win.
Help us to remember
that it was Your light that set You out
not just Your lightness,
it's the light of love that lifts us
it's the weight of fear and guilt that pull us down,
not shoes, not gadgets.
If they get in the way,
give us wisdom to leave them by the road
but help us to remember
help us to understand
that that is not enough.

Suggested Readings

Matthew 6:19–21	*Lay up treasures in heaven*
Acts 4:32–35	*Christ's followers held everything in common*

Blessing

> Bless my possessions, Lord,
> bless the things I own
> may I use them for good
> to give and to share
> and for all the purposes of love.

PATIENCE

Now there was a man in Jerusalem whose name was Simeon; this man was righteous and devout, looking forward to the consolation of Israel, and the Holy Spirit rested on him. It had been revealed to him by the Holy Spirit that he would not see death before he had seen the Lord's Messiah.

~ Luke 2:25–26 ~

Meditation

Time to wait –
and in the waiting
watch the faces come and go,
as they have grown from childlike wonder
through the storm, tantrum and question
of middle years
to aging wisdom
etched in lines across the skin.

Time to wait –
and the story of love has been
rehearsed and repeated
in the worship and living
of those for whom it was told.

Time to wait –
and play a part in the workings
of the world around
but yet know
that in God's time
He responds to our deepest desires
with the fulfilment of His promises.

Prayer

Lord of all time and space,
with the sun set in the sky
and the moon and stars placed upon the heavens,
You named the changing pattern of light
as 'day' and 'night'.

In work, play and rest,
You offer space and opportunities
to find You in all aspects of life.
In the midst of Your space and time
we set out limits
so that we might scurry
from one activity to another
failing to stop and wonder
at all that surrounds.
As we seek You in our busy-ness,
make us patient enough to wait,
and discover that pleasure
is to be found in anticipation –
in the not having all and doing everything –
but simply waiting on Your presence.   AMEN.

Suggested Readings

1 Thessalonians 5:12–28   *Instructions for living*
Luke 2:21–38   *Jesus presented at the Temple*

Blessing

God of patience,
may thoughts be calmed,
anxieties lifted
and activity rested,
as Your promise is awaited –
this day and always.   AMEN.

KINDNESS

As God's chosen ones, holy and beloved, clothe yourselves with compassion, kindness, humility, meekness, and patience.

~ Colossians 3:12 ~

Meditation

Not nice –
not sweet –
not generous –
but kind.

Kindness gives from what it has
and not from what it can afford;
it is never too busy
to notice the needs of others
and never too shy to admonish others
with empathy and love;
it kindles the fires of compassion
and turns companions into kindred;
it participates in the lives of others
without being intrusive
and sows the seeds that only bear good fruit.

Not soft –
not friendly –
not lenient –
but kind.

Prayer

Gracious God,
teach me that kindness is more
than a word in my vocabulary
or a thought in my mind.

Show me that kindness is an act
that comes from my heart –
which moves me
to put the needs of others
before myself.

Help me to discover for myself,
however slowly
and however tentatively,
a spirit of kindness that
is gentle and generous,
loving and forgiving
to all those I meet.

Prepare me for the challenges
that being clothed in kindness brings;
that I may find the courage
to speak the truth in love
and pursue justice in the face of hatred.   AMEN.

Suggested Readings

Galatians 5:22–26   *Fruits of the Spirit*
Ephesians 4:31–32   *Rules for new life*

Blessing

May the beauty of God
be reflected in your heart,
the wisdom of God
be reflected in your words,
the love of God
be reflected in your hands
and the kindness of God
reflected through your soul.   AMEN.

ENVY

The children struggled together within her; and she said, 'If it is to be this way, why do I live?' So she went to enquire of the Lord. And the Lord said to her, 'Two nations are in your womb, and two peoples born of you shall be divided; the one shall be stronger than the other, the elder shall serve the younger.'

~ Genesis 25:22–23 ~

Meditation

Discontent engulfs the space between
the differing personalities,
for in the opposing
lies the qualities, the achievements,
the ambition, the personality,
the possessions that are hoped for.
Envy eats away
pervading through pores
as hatred heightens
and clouds the vision
of the human being behind the characteristics.
Ears blocked to the common bindings.
Eyes closed to the pain of others.
Hands clasped lest touching
might narrow the gap between.

Christ stands in the midst,
preparing the meal that heals divisions
where the bread of peace
and the cup of unity
pull diversity together
in the Heavenly Kingdom.

Prayer

Embracing Lord,
You seek to draw all people together
in Your love,
drawing on the strengths and weaknesses
of all who follow.

We instead see the gifts of another
as a potential threat to our position or living.
Help us to recognise
that each of us is given gifts
that have a place in the building of Your community.
Remind us that what we might consider worthless
is often just what You were seeking.
So may Your Spirit
burst through the barriers we have created
and pull together what we offer
so that the picture of Christ
in the midst of life
is revealed in the combined action.   AMEN.

Suggested Readings

> Genesis 25:19–34   *Birth right*
> Luke 15:11–32   *Prodigal Son/Loving Father*

Blessing

> Lord, bless our differences for they shape
> how we might tell Your story.
> Christ, break our barriers
> when we cannot see the common ground.
> Holy Spirit, lead us to explore how
> we might work together.   AMEN.

BOASTFULNESS

Let each of us please his neighbour for his good, to build him up.

~ Romans 15:2 ~

Meditation

It happens almost without me noticing,
a snag in my throat
a prickle in my palms,
the urge to say
to tell everyone
to drop, lightly, into the conversation,
I did that too
I did that better
I did so many things
I am exactly the kind of person
you'd have to admire.

This desire to proclaim my feats
flows down my body
until I'm lifting my feet from the floor with
a pile of crammed announcements of
books I've read,
ideas I've had,
people I've met,
things I own,
things I've given away.
Even the achievements of
my family, my friends
are stomped below my feet,
to raise my head above those around me,
to keep my head above the water
of my oceanic insecurity.

Prayer

Jesus, boastfulness is such a clear failing –
we know that those who have something to show
have nothing to prove.
And yet we find ourselves clutching

as drowning women and men
to the things that make us stand taller
the things that set us above our peers.

Boasting is an act of bravado in theory,
but often an act of desperation in practice.
Jesus, Son of the Creator,
perfect and perfecting friend and leader,
You had more to boast of
than anyone who ever walked on earth,
yet You chose no crown,
no cloth of gold,
Your brilliant and impressive words
all pointed to God, to heaven,
to our path to freedom.

Give us the confidence in You, Lord,
the confidence to know that You made us well
that we are loved and above all
we are liked by the Messiah Himself –
from top to toe –
help us to stay rooted to the ground.
Let us love and build up the ground that others stand on,
and so help them ever heavenward,
keep them ever above the waters of fear.

Suggested Readings

> Romans 15:1–6   *The example of Christ*
> Matthew 6:1–7   *Introducing the Lord's Prayer*

Blessing

> Forbid it, Lord, that I should boast,
> Save in the death of Christ my God!
> All the vain things that charm me most,
> I sacrifice them to His blood.
>
> *When I survey the wondrous cross* – Isaac Watts

ARROGANCE

For all who exalt themselves will be humbled,
but all who humble themselves will be exalted.

~ Luke 18:14b ~

Meditation

There I was in all my finery.
Right up there
with the best of them.
Right up there
making a show of myself.
Right up there
safe in the knowledge
of what it takes to make an impression
when it matters.

But my plastic piety
was as see through
as the interlaced fingers
of my transparent prayers.
And I found myself
slipping through the gaps
in my argument
with nowhere soft to land.

And there I was exposed.
Right down there
with the worst of them.
Right down there
with nothing to show.
Right down there
safe in the knowledge
that nothing impresses as much
as knowing what truly matters.

Prayer

Lord, we seek stallions
while You unrope a donkey.
We expect fanfares
while You slip quietly away.
We limit love to those who love us
while You dish it out
to anyone and everyone.
We measure our faith
not by our own inaction
but by the actions of others.

And yet we have the cheek
to call ourselves Your people.
We dare to believe
that we do enough to merit Your grace.

Help us to step back
and take a long hard look
at what You expect of us.
Only then may we be ready
to come into Your presence.
In Jesus' name we pray.   AMEN.

Suggested Readings

Luke 18:9–14   *Parable of the Pharisee and the tax collector*
James 3:13–18   *Harvest of righteousness*

Blessing

Bless us in our standing back
that we might see You better.
Bless us in our holding back
that we might share You more.
Bless us in our uncertainty
that we might know You fully.
Bless us in our going out
that we might meet You on the road.   AMEN.

RUDENESS

*Those who passed by derided him, shaking their heads and saying,
'You who would destroy the temple and build it in three days, save
yourself!'*

~ Matthew 27:39–40a ~

Meditation

Love is not rude.

Love stands naked
while the rude
are clothed in shame.

Neither blood red robe,
nor crown of contempt
nor sceptre of cynicism
can make opaque
such transparent goodness.

Love retains dignity
while the rude
are an affront to themselves.

Neither ignorant insults,
nor spiteful spittle
nor berating blows
can make unseemly
such stature of grace.

Love is lifted high
while the rude
descend to degradation.

Neither passer-by put downs,
nor religious ridicule
nor crudeness of cross companions
can bring low
the One who is Love.

The ultimate rudeness
is the derision and crucifixion of Love.

Prayer

I know You have told me
to love others as You love me
yet still
I can be so rude:

ignoring questions that annoy
putting down those who disagree with me,
showing irritation to those who need more time,
silencing the child who disrupts my plans,
diminishing those who threaten me,
deriding those whom I do not understand,
rejecting those who try to help
and being rudest of all
to the ones who love me most.

Regardless of another's race or faith or age,
regardless of another's gender or sexuality,
regardless of – my perception of –
another's attraction, intelligence and ability
help me to honour the dignity,
respect the personhood
and love the Christ
in everyone I meet   AMEN.

Suggested Scripture Readings

Matthew 27:27–44   *The rudeness of humanity to God*
Luke 7:36–50   *The Pharisee's rudeness to Jesus*

Blessing

May the grace of our Lord Jesus Christ,
the love of God
and the fellowship of the Holy Spirit
be not only
with You
but with all You meet.   AMEN.

INSISTING ON ITS OWN WAY

Jesus said to him, 'I am the way, and the truth, and the life. No one comes to the Father except through me.'

~ John 14:6 ~

Meditation

If I look hard enough …
staring back at me in the depths of the screen
I see a reflection,
of someone I once knew.
A smile flickers as
moments of laughter and deep abiding joy
are but fleeting moments of the past.

I waste away in the depths of Sheol
wallowing in the insistence, that
my way IS the way
but there, You find me
and there, You show me
the way to begin again
hallowed be Your name.

Prayer

How wrong we get it, God.
When we think that we can do it
My Way, Sinatra style
and then when the lights go up,
the cracks begin to show.
God guide us back to You.
Show us Your way.
Help us to see it
as, our way.
Me and You, God,
I'm ready
to stop insisting
and start listening …
to You.   AMEN.

Suggested Readings

Job 16:17–22   *The way of no return*
Acts 27   *Paul, on the way to Damascus*

Blessing

May God guard you through every trouble.
May God guide you through the complexity of life.
And may the way
be open to you
Today and every day.   Amen.

IRRITABILITY

As God's chosen ones, holy and beloved, clothe yourselves with compassion, kindness, humility, meekness and patience.

~ Colossians 3:12 ~

Meditation

That's a tall order, God:
compassion
kindness
humility
meekness
patience.

I don't know if I will ever make it
on all five counts.
I might just manage to be
compassionate and kind,
or humble and meek
but never all at the same time.

And there's one I'll never get:
patience.

I just get so frustrated:
at myself,
at others,
when I just can't put my finger on it.

I can be so irksome
and yes, irritable
if I am honest with You, God.

I say something I'll live to regret.
I'll chuck it in before I've even started.

Sometimes, I wonder
if You might feel the same way about me?
I wouldn't blame You if You did.

But then, You remind me of everything else:
compassion
kindness

humility
meekness
patience.

You've got it all God.
I'll settle for just a little bit.
One
    Day
        At
           A
              Time.

Prayer

Forgive me God
for the things I do and say
when I don't make the time or space.

For compassion, kindness, humility, meekness
and patience.

Teach me to learn from You
and to set aside all
that makes me
irritable.

And yes, irritating too!
Because God, You call me
as I am
to be Yours.   AMEN.

Suggested Readings

        Proverbs 29   *Simple but wise words*
    Galatians 5:22–26   *The fruits of the Spirit*

Blessing

        Let silence be woven to your lips.
        May your mind and heart
        be stilled, just as Jesus stilled the storm.
        May the tumult within you cease.
        And may you be embraced with God's love
        and peace.

RESENTFULNESS

Ahab went home resentful and sullen because of what Naboth the Jezreelite had said to him.

~ 1 Kings 21:4 ~

Meditation

Some have everything a person could want,
certainly more than anyone could need,
enough to lavish on their own
all kinds of worldly goods
and yet it doesn't seem to be enough.

Some have everything they will ever need,
enough to eat, drink and be merry
and to feed their own
in body, mind and soul
and yet it doesn't seem to be enough.

Some have everything to satisfy their need;
they get by day by day,
able to still their hunger
and slake their thirst,
enough to fill their children's bellies
with good things
and yet it doesn't seem to be enough.

And there are those who have not enough,
those who cannot eat their fill,
those who cannot give to their own
the things that hold together
body and soul.
For them, plainly, it is not enough.

All kinds of people in our world,
divided in their differences
and yet united in one thing:
they see what belongs to their neighbours
and covet.

How long, O Lord? How long?
Must this be so for ever?

Prayer

Lord God,
it's hard not to be resentful
when we see others enjoying
the things they have – and we don't.
Even if we never suffer
just one day of hunger in our lives,
even if we never feel the lack of water
or of anything else we need,
we still want more and more each day,
no matter the cost to others.

Forgive us, Lord and remind us
of Your call to love.
To love You
and to love our neighbours,
our enemies
and our close ones,
just as we love ourselves.

And remind us at the beginning and ending
of every day
that we love because
You first loved us.
In Jesus' name we pray.   AMEN.

Suggested Readings

      1 Kings 21:1–16   *Naboth's Vineyard*
    Ecclesiastes 5:13–20   *Do not be resentful*

Blessing

        May the blessings of
        God's peace and contentment
        rest upon you
        and on those whom you love,
        this and every day.   AMEN.

REJOICING IN WRONGDOING

Now the betrayer had given them a sign, saying, 'the one I will kiss is the man, arrest him'.

~ Matthew 26:48 ~

Meditation

You've got no idea
how good it feels
to have money in my pocket.

You see, he had taken it all away
from me
with those words, 'Follow me.'

And I did. Lord knows
why I did
follow him.
My life, my livelihood,
my all
and for what?
Abuse, derisive stares
the local board of examiners
waiting to fail us.

I've got my future for me now
in cold, hard cash
money beyond my wildest dreams.

So
why does it feel like
I've paid the price?

I should be rejoicing
but I'm not.
Oh Jesus, what have I done
to You?

Prayer

Forgive us Lord
for we have failed You.
We choose our own paths.
'What's in it for me?'
is the first question on our lips.

Loving God,
redirect our lives.
Lead us in Your ways
so that we may truly rejoice
always, with You.   AMEN.

Suggested Readings

I John 2:7–17   *A new commandment*
Romans 13:1–10   *Being subject to God's authority*

Blessing

May this day be a blessing to you.
May you be a blessing to others.
May you put right what's wrong
and in so doing
may God bless you abundantly
and all shall be well.   AMEN.

REJOICING IN THE TRUTH

I have no greater joy than this, to hear that my children are walking in the truth.

~ 3 John 1:4 ~

Meditation

The truth calls us
by a new name into new places,
frees our lips to sing heartsongs,
fills our arms with unexpected bundles of joy.

The truth claims us
from a place of darkness,
points towards a shaft of light
in cracked and broken lives
and whispers 'no going back'.

The truth challenges us
with barefaced brazenness,
draws a line in the sand
and dares us to step over
into uncharted territory.

The truth hurts,
lays itself bare,
pierces souls with its honesty,
squeezes out the last drop
of love from its wounds
and bleeds itself dry
so we might walk rejoicing
that the truth is out.

Prayer

The truth is, Lord,
we're not as honest as we like to think.
We deceive ourselves
when we call our actions holy.
We trick ourselves

into thinking that our will is Yours.
We hide our hand and double deal You.
Yet believe it or not, Lord, we love You.
Not as deeply, as completely,
as unconditionally as You love us
but enough to know
that Yours is the way we want to live.

Help us, Lord, to be true to You
and to ourselves that we might
serve with integrity
love with sincerity
and so share the reality of You.   AMEN.

Suggested Readings

> 3 John 1   *Co-workers with the truth*
> John 14:6–7   *The way, the truth and the life*

Blessing

> The way, may we walk it in faith.
> The truth, may we speak it with sincerity.
> The life, may we live it through grace
> so our hearts may be open to love.   AMEN.

BEARING ALL THINGS

Bear one another's burdens and in this way you will fulfil the law of Christ.

~ Galatians 6:2 ~

Meditation

I cannot bear all things.
I have tried
and I have failed.
But you, St Paul
have shown me the error
of my ways.

It is LOVE
that can bear all things.

Even You, Christ,
did not bear all things alone.
You needed the love of
family, friends and disciples.
And when it was too much to bear
in Gethsemane, on Golgotha,
carrying the weight of the world
on Your shoulders
God's love carried You,
His precious Son.

It is Love alone
that can bear all things.

Yet we cannot love alone.
For love is relationship,
is giving and receiving.
So help me share
in bearing all things Lord,
joining heart and hands with others
to carry life itself.

Prayer

Loving Lord,
may all who can no longer endure

their responsibilities
or their circumstances
hear Jesus say:
'Come to me all you that are weary
and carrying heavy burdens':
those who feel the weight of illness
or the weight of care for one who is ill;
those who feel the pressure of work
or the pressure of no work:
those who bear the millstone of grief
or the millstone of guilt;
those who suffer daily persecution
or daily abuse;
those who carry hunger in their bodies
or hunger in their souls;
those individuals or groups
whom we name before You now ...
'Come to me,
and I will give you rest.'
Lord, when we ourselves
are tested beyond our means,
give us the humble faith
to come to You
but also to recognise
that Your help
still comes in human form.   AMEN.

Suggested Readings

Galatians 6:1–5   *Bear one another's burdens*
Matthew 11:28–30   *Jesus' call to the burdened*

Blessing

May Christ's yoke fit easily upon you.
May His burden be ever light.
May His love gentle your heart.
And may you be blessed
by the One who endures all things.   AMEN.

BELIEVING ALL THINGS

Jesus said to him, 'Have you believed because you have seen me?
Blessed are those who have not seen and yet have come to believe.'

~ John 20:29 ~

Meditation

I have never seen the tooth fairy
nor Christmas Santa in my house.
But I believe because I find
the evidence they left behind.

In God I trust with child's faith
and Jesus loves me, this I know.
Yes, I believe because I hear
the story told convincingly.

By teenage years myths are undone,
science and reason joust with Scripture
What can I believe if I do not find
the evidence I seek?

Yet as adult I've met the Prodigal son
and the good Samaritan many times.
I believe in Love's transforming power
that no science can explain.

In later years, beliefs well-worn:
I've seen birth and dying and life.
And I believe the Risen Christ
has walked and talked with me.

Yes I believe my Lord, my God
all things are possible for You ...

Prayer

Dear Lord,
Did Thomas put his hand into Your side,
after his confession of faith?
I've often wondered.

You invite me to the blessing
of believing without beholding.

But I've seen everyday miracle:
in the new born baby,
in the first snowdrop of Spring,
in the face of one forgiven.

And the invitation
to reach inside Your wounds
still whispers in the wind.
For Your woundedness is our woundedness.

Dear Lord,
please give me the courage and compassion
to respond when invited
to reach inside: the pain
of another's bereavement,
or dementia, or depression,
or terminal illness or chronic loneliness
or self-rejection.
Give me the first words of miracle:
'I am here for you. I love you'.

Lord, I believe that nothing and no one
is beyond Love's redemption.
So I guess that means:
I believe all things.

Suggested Readings

John 20:24–30   *Blessed are those who believe the whole
                  story*
Acts 24:10–21   *Paul defends his faith before the Roman
                  Governor*

Blessing

> May your belonging be blessed:
> you are God's child.
> May your behaving be blessed:
> you are Christ's presence in the world.
> May your believing be blessed:
> you are the Spirit's channel.   AMEN.

HOPING ALL THINGS

And now, O Lord, what do I wait for? My hope is in you.

~ Psalm 39:7 ~

Meditation

Four letters.
One word.
One syllable.
How such a small thing
can contain the hugeness
of promise and possibility
of dream and desire
of aspiration and anticipation
of expectation and risk
would take sentences galore to explain
and still not be enough.

And yet those
four letters
one word
one syllable
begins with the smallest of things.
The fluttering
in a barren womb,
the space between
a hesitant hand
and a passing cloak,
the first tug
at death's bindings,
the glint of fish scales
on a beach
are just enough.

Four letters.
One word.
One syllable
are quite enough
to say it all.

Prayer

Lord, You asked us
to pin all our hopes on You
then hung Yourself from a cross
and left us with only words.
Lord, You asked us
to wait for You

and went on ahead
to a place we couldn't explain.
Yet we thank You for giving us
enough glimpses of love to cling to,
for answering our complexity
with Your simplicity,
for giving meaning
to the littleness of our lives.
And we thank You that there
is still more to be learned
about the depths of Your grace.

We are waiting, Lord.
Just say the word.

Suggested Readings

Psalm 39 *A prayer of hope*
Romans 8:24–25 *Waiting in hope*

Blessing

May you trip over truth
and fall headlong into hope.
May redemption rain down all around you.
May God's glory catch you napping
and God's story catch your breath
and God's gratuity perpetually astound you.

Prodigal Blessing, Spoken Worship – Gerard Kelly

ENDURING ALL THINGS

And remember, I am with you always, to the end of the age.

~ Matthew 28:20b ~

Meditation

Nothing lasts, we told him.
Nets tangle.
Boats rot.
Children grow.
Dreams die.

Nothing lasts, we were warned.
Words fade.
Popularity wanes.
Chances are lost.
Journeys end.

Nothing lasts and we knew it.
In the tension of bread broken.
In the bitter summons of dawn.
On a bloodied tree.
In the stench of a tomb.

And just when there was nothing
but life-limiting memories
and might-have-beens
something became clear.
That we had everything.
Nothing lasts, He told us,
like love.

Prayer

We're not as hard wearing
as we like to think, Lord.
Once, like the disciples,
we might have cast aside careers
to skirt the water's edge
and teeter on mountain tops;

lived off crumbs of comfort
while grasping at thin dreams.
But life has softened us
and forever and ever
slips easily off our tongues.

Lord, when we become too used
to the guarantees that come
wrapped up in eternity,
remind us of what You endured
that we might be remade
in Your eternal, everlasting grace.   AMEN.

Suggested Readings

> Matthew 28:18–20   *The Great Commission*
> Hebrews 10:32–36   *Great reward*

Blessing

> Show to us in everything we touch
> and everyone we meet
> the continued assurance
> of Thy presence round us
> lest we should ever think Thee absent.

The Glory in the Grey – The Whole Earth Shall Cry Glory
– Revd George F. MacLeod

LOVE NEVER ENDS

The steadfast love of the Lord never ceases,
his mercies never come to an end.

~ Lamentations 3:22 ~

Meditation

When I was little, I was loved.
Love surrounded me and held me,
flowing from those who came before me,
who shared my blood.
To them, I was most precious,
longed for and loved.

When I grew, I was loved.
Love nurtured me and blessed me,
flowing from those who taught me,
who instructed me about the world
and its ways.
To them, I was full of promise,
the hope for tomorrow.

When I was grown, I was loved.
Love found me and captured me,
flowing from another
and making us one.
Love helped us create
and bear fruit.
Then, I was joy and fulfilment,
I was at the centre
of someone's world.

When I was old, I was loved.
Love upheld me with kindness
and care,
flowing from those bound to me
by ties of family
and friendship.
To them, I was warmth
and wisdom and love.

Now that I'm gone, still I am loved.
Utter Love embraces me,
flowing from Him who holds all
in His arms,
Who sustains all
by His breath.
To Him, Who is Love,
I am precious
and longed for and loved.

Prayer

Lord,
Is this how it was meant to be,
love from our first breath to our last
and beyond?
But in our broken world life doesn't often
turn out this way.
In our fallenness we forget to love,
we forget to let ourselves be loved
and we forget to love You.
It seems that our love does end.
Help us, Lord, to remember
day by day
that Your love is for ever.
And when we forget,
remind us that there is always
a way back to You,
for Jesus' sake. AMEN

Suggested Readings

John 3:16–21 *God so loved the world*
I John 4:7–21 *God is love*

Blessing

May the love of God,
true, pure and freely given,
uphold me every moment,
so that love can flow
through me to those around me
constantly.

ENDINGS

Now when the Lord was about to take Elijah up to heaven by a whirlwind, Elijah and Elisha were on their way from Gilgal.

~ 2 Kings 2:1 ~

Meditation

What is an ending but the opportunity of a new beginning?

That doesn't mean
it won't hurt
or cause heartache
or bring relief or a flurry of excitement.

It doesn't mean
there won't be anguish,
or grief,
or pain,
or joy,
or hope,
or a time of change.

In every ending,
there is something new that awaits
and in faith
we grasp the hands that pull us forward
trusting that they will shape what is to come.

Prayer

Lord of each moment,
it can be easy to be comfortable with life
and to take the way things are
and have been,
for granted.
So when the whirlwind of change sweeps through
it is not surprising
that we find ourselves cast adrift
on our waves of emotion.

May we allow Your Spirit
to settle upon us,
leading us from old ways
to new hopes,
assured that in every ending
that there is the opportunity
to explore something new of God.   AMEN.

Suggested Readings

   2 Kings 2:1–14   *Elijah passes his role as prophet to
Elisha*
   Mark 16:1–8   *The women discover the empty tomb*

Blessing

God of the beginning and the end,
Alpha and Omega,
may You bless us as we travel from the old to the new;
may the words of Christ call us from old patterns to new
    ideas;
and may the Holy Spirit hold us
when we are afraid to leave what we know
to discover what we might become.   AMEN.

CHILDISHNESS

*So Christ himself gave the apostles, the prophets, the evangelists,
the pastors and teachers, to equip his people for works of service,
so that the body of Christ may be built up until we all reach unity in
the faith and in the knowledge of the Son of God and become mature,
attaining to the whole measure of the fullness of Christ.*

~ Ephesians 4:11–13 ~

Meditation

I strive to grow
I hope to grow through a long life,
to become a better daughter,
boyfriend, wife,
brother, friend, person, Christian.
A better follower of Christ.

I have grown up
I am a grown-up.
Madam and not miss.
Sir and not son.

How do I measure that?
Pencil marks on a door frame?
Responsibility for myself and others?
Is it a shift in what I want,
or do I still make the same old demands?
Do I still throw the same old tantrums?

Let me think now for a minute
of the changes in me from my childhood to now.
Which of those were good and Godly
and which weren't?

Prayer

My Lord, my Father, my Teacher,
You lived with us
the King of heaven who chose
to be surrounded by our childishness:

the catty squabbling and attention seeking
of the apostles,
our noisy, self-centred lives today.
iPod, iPhone, I want, I need.

But by walking with us, then and now,
You present us with another model of maturity,
adulthood not taught by celebrity or catalogues,
by banking systems or traditions.
Your adulthood is measured by insight,
self-sacrifice,
a desire for the truth,
calm, peace, enjoyment and faith.
It does not demand to walk alone,
it relies on the companionship and support
of friends, family, community and our King.

Lord, help us to become grown-ups
in our faith and in our life.
May we attain to the whole measure of You,
the depths of Your patience
and the heights of Your love.

Suggested Readings

Ephesians 4:1–16   *Unity and maturity in the body of
Christ*
2 Timothy 2:22–26   *Flee the evil desires of youth*

Blessing

May we act as the grown-ups you want us to be:
healing more than we hurt,
providing more than we demand
and loving more than anything at all.   AMEN.

CHILDLIKENESS

*Truly I tell you, whoever does not receive the kingdom of God as a
little child will never enter it.*

~ Mark 10:15 ~

Reflection

My pulse races
and my heart flutters with excitement
as, in wonder and amazement, I stand
with eyes wide open
and mouth agape.

You rekindle my imagination;
You reawaken my sense of awe;
You restore in me a playful Spirit;
as You revive my hopes
and remind me that my dreams are possible.

Whatever age I may be
You bring out the child in me.
For next to You, I am:
forever young,
willing to trust,
eager to learn,
and excited by each new discovery I make.

You remind me that I am never
fully grown-up,
but always growing up;
and growing closer,
step by step,
day by day,
to You and Your kingdom.

Prayer

Grant me, O God,
the wisdom to realise
that I can't always:

bear all things
understand all things
be in control.

Help me to realise
that it's not weak:
to ask for help
to say 'I don't understand'
to need a hug.

Help me to open my mind
to the joy of new experiences.

Awaken me to the possibilities
of new discoveries and adventures.

Enfold me in the arms of Your love
and remind me that I am always
Your precious child.   AMEN.

Suggested Readings

Mark 9:36–37   *Who is the greatest?*
Mark 10:13–16   *Jesus blesses children*

Blessing

Now I lay me down to sleep,
I pray the Lord my soul to keep.
Let angels watch me through the night
and wake me with the morning light.   AMEN.

SEEING IN A MIRROR, DIMLY

And all of us, with unveiled faces, seeing the glory of the Lord, as though reflected in a mirror, are being transformed into the same image from one degree of glory to another;

~ 2 Corinthians 3:18a ~

Meditation

Longing to see Your glory,
day and night I pray and polish –
'Mirror, mirror on the wall
where is the Fairest of them all?'
But the image remains dim
and You, God of loving justice,
appear shrouded in a haze.

Longing to be a good disciple,
I listen to the Gospel's message
thinking I understand Jesus' command
to love others as He loves me.
Yet often I seem to live and do otherwise.
If only, I could solve the riddle –
how to glimpse You more clearly?

Longing to see Your glory,
day and night I pray and polish –
until a light dawns – just one brief flash –
Oh God!
Dear God.
It's not the mirror that needs polishing.
It's me.
I who am made in Your image
but reflect You so dimly.

Forgive me Lord.
Polish me Lord.
Until I can bare to see myself.
And in my transparency let others see You too.

Prayer

Loving God,
polish us into the sacramental mirror

of baptism
where Your grace is poured out
in the symbol of water and in Spirit
and we remember that Your offer of love
is for everyone.

Sacrificial God,
polish us into the sacramental mirror
of communion
where Jesus' faithfulness sets the table
and we remember that Christ is made known
in the breaking of bread with friend and stranger
and in every act of self-giving.

Living God,
polish us into the sacramental mirror
of Easter Morning
when Your glory blazes upon the earth
and we remember that You have conquered death
and that Jesus is seen in every resurrection,
in every raising up of those who are fallen or trampled.
AMEN.

Suggested Readings

2 Corinthians 3:12–18   *Turn to the Lord for brightness*
James 1:19–27   *Dim mirrors if hearing and
not doing*

Blessing

Just as water reflects the human face
so one human heart reflects another.

Proverbs 27:19

Bless my heart Lord that it may reflect Your love,
bless my neighbour's heart that it may reflect Your love
that in all our neighbourly doings
we may be of one heart – Yours –
and Your face may be glimpsed upon the earth.   AMEN.

SEEING FACE TO FACE

Thus the Lord used to speak to Moses, face to face; as one speaks to a friend.

~ Exodus 33:11 ~

Meditation

Face to face, Lord,
You spoke to Moses
in the intimacy of Friendship.

A sharing of mutual love
and concern for all Your people –
dare I presume such intimacy?

Side by side, Lord,
I believe that You walk with me
in our journey of Friendship.

Hand in hand, Lord,
I trust that You act with me
in our mission of Friendship.

Heart to heart, Lord
I pray that You love with me
in our communion of Friendship.

Face to face, Lord,
I hope You will meet with me
in a revelation of Friendship

but only
when You judge me ready
to be face to face
with Perfect Love.

Prayer

Dear Lord,
maybe we try too hard
to pitch our tents of meeting
for face-to-face confrontations:
across war councils or election campaigns,
across boardrooms or debating parlours,

across kitchens tables or doorsteps.
Help us to pitch
our tents of meeting with You:
in places where division exists
between rich and poor,
between warring nations,
between abuser and abused
between those of different faiths.
May the presence of Your Spirit
enable us to walk side by side
in a journey of partnership.
May the person of Jesus,
teach us to work hand in hand
in a battle against poverty.
And may the power of Your love
compel us to connect heart to heart
in an embrace of the lost and lonely.

Then side by side,
hand in hand and heart to heart,
in the meeting tent of Your world
may we see ourselves
face to face with Your reflection.

Suggested Readings

Exodus 33:7–11 *God speaks to Moses in the meeting tent*
John 11:28–36 *Jesus weeps and the Jews see the face*
of love

Blessing

May God's companionship
be your constant.
May God's work
be your lifetime.
May God's love
be your produce.
And may Christ who
laid down His life for His friends
bring You safely home
to face Your Maker.   AMEN.

BEING FULLY KNOWN

Even before a word is on my tongue, O Lord, you know it completely.

~ Psalm 139:4 ~

Meditation

We hide.
As human beings, we hide.
We cannot get a few chapters through the Bible
before people are hiding
from the Lord
from each other
from themselves;
hiding the perfection of created bodies
hiding the truth about their cruelty and greed.

How often do we feel like Adam and Eve,
crouched in the undergrowth,
in a pointless game of hide and seek
with the King Creator?
Heart pounding, trying with all our might
to stay unseen,
unknown.
But we are already unearthed,
there is nowhere we can bury ourselves
without God.
We need not fear the sharp glare
of the interrogator's lamp,
because we are already bathing in the warmth,
the care, of the sun,
the all-pervading Light of the World.

Prayer

Father, I am afraid to let You into the deepest,
the darkest parts of me.
The thought of laying open
my heart, my past, my mind to You
fills me with terror.
But You know.

You know exactly.
Even these words of fear, forming on my tongue,
are known by You, are loved by You.
You are in the air into which I speak,
on the page onto which I write,
in the zeros and ones through which I type.
You are there waiting for the words You know will come
holding them,
cupping them
while they are still in the depths of my soul.
Let me think now of the things I try to hide,
to spread them out for You,
remembering
there is nothing for You to discover,
You have known them,
known them all
and You take my hand anyway and say,

It is you I love. You.
Warts and words and all.

Suggested Readings

Psalm 139   *The inescapable God*
1 Samuel 16:7   *God speaks to Samuel*

Blessing

Known and therefore loved,
Loved and therefore known,
may the miracle of Your understanding,
guide and hold me
day by day.   AMEN.

ABIDING

*But as his anointing teaches you about all things, and is true and is
not a lie, and just as it has taught you, abide in him.*

~ 1 John 2:27 ~

Meditation

They call it a catafalque –
where the coffin rests.
I read about that last time I was in
the crematorium waiting room.

It all seems too familiar.
I suppose I have reached that stage in my life
when it is inevitable that some of my friends
will die before me.
It just seems to be happening
too frequently for my liking.

And yet there is something there
beneath the well-rehearsed script
of platitudes
volleyed by friends and family.

There's a certainty in the minister's eye,
a passion in her voice
that plants a seed of hope
in this garden of desolation
that is life and death.

Abide with me – that's the one.
It just captures me
that sense of deep abiding love
that knows no end.

I'd like some of that, God.
That's all I can say.
So, abide with me
and I, in You.

Prayer

It's not easy to have faith in You, God
when the walls of my life seem to be
closing in.

And yet sometimes it is there, You are there.
You lift me up from life's lowest ebb
and You carry me forward.
And all I can say is
thank You Lord for not leaving me
as I've left You before.

So abide with me
and I, in You.   AMEN.

Suggested Readings

Psalm 90	*The everlasting God*
Revelation 20	*The book of life*

Blessing

As you are in the ebb and flow of life,
as the beginning becomes the ending,
the ending is a new beginning.
So may the blessing of God be ever with you
today and every day.   AMEN.

Twelve Additional Monthly Prayers

LOVE OF CREATION

Creator God,
You spun the substance of light into stars
and laid them across the sky in splendour.
You painted the vermilion sunset
and hung it over the cerulean sea.
You sculpted the craggy mountains
and dusted them in snow.
You moulded the deepest oceans
and filled them with life-giving waters.
You wove the multi-coloured tapestry of land
and laid it like a quilt over the earth.

And then into it all You poured
all the riches of nature
and all the wonders of life.

And it was good.
It was loved.
It contained and reflected something
of Your very nature and being.

I marvel at Your composition,
which fills my ears with sweet song.
I delight in Your artistry,
which brings beauty to my eyes.
I sense the rhythm of the seasons
in the warmth of the Summer sun;
the crispness of an Autumn breeze.
I contemplate the myriad of stars
and feel humbled to be part of it all.

Ever present, yet ever changing;
You surround me with reminders
of Your love for all things under the Heavens.

Help me to be a good steward
of this world's riches;
respectful towards those from whose lands

resources are extracted;
responsible for my own impact on nature;
and ever mindful of my responsibilities
towards those who suffer most
from environmental harm.

Help me not to take this world for granted;
but to cherish it with the same love
that You have poured
into every grain of sand,
each blade of grass,
and every cell of me.   AMEN.

Suggested Prayer Activity

You may wish to read through Psalm 23.
Visualise the green pastures and the still waters.

Take some time to pray in an outside space – this may be your own garden, a local park, or farther afield. Try and pick a time when human traffic and noise are at a minimum.

Once you have picked your spot, make yourself as comfortable as possible and take time to tune into the natural world around you. Take a few moments to reflect not just on what you can see; but also on what you can hear, what you can smell and what you can feel; whether that's the sound of birds singing in the trees or the feel of a light breeze upon your face. Once you feel that you have captured an image of your surroundings try and express these feelings in your prayers.

You may also like to read through the story of creation in Genesis 1. Give thanks for each part of creation reflecting on how that part affects your daily life.

EROS AND LUST

Where is love in lust, Lord?
Love, the holiest of holies,
where is it in page three,
or freezing Saturday nightclub queues?
But then, where is it in the Bible itself
in the urgency and desire of
the Song of Songs?
How can I tell the difference
between love,
pleasure,
need,
demands?
How can I pick my path between what I want
what You want
and what the world wants?
In our past we see shame that closed life down,
that shunned women and men,
that labelled lust the deepest, darkest of sins
for generations,
and yet, the way we live now
it too can feel like imprisonment.
Who, what and how I should want
are barked at me from films, TVs, websites,
self-help books, magazines, targeted ads
to hit me between the eyes
with all the condescension and conscription
of slavery.

Lord, we give thanks for the gift of lust;
give us the wisdom to treat it with respect
and give us strength to trust that
closeness
intimacy
and
passion
will reign.

King of the Passion,
May our passion be for one another,
to salve and serve,
to join and rejoice,
and may every single breath
be hallelujah.

Suggested Prayer Activity

> *You may like to read through Song of Solomon chapter 2.*
>
> Why do you think this book was included in the canon of the Holy Scriptures?
>
> Is there any way in which God's love for humanity could be considered as romantic?
>
> Are there great romantic love stories in books or films or the lives of others that have moved and inspired you over the years? Give thanks for the gift of romance. Pray for young people that they may experience genuine romantic love and not only sexual encounters. You may wish also to pray for older people who feel that romance is dead in their own lives.
>
> As a contrast, read through the story of David's lustful possession of Bathsheba (*2 Samuel 11 and 12*). We are often most shocked by the infidelities of those in positions of public trust and those in the media spotlight. Pray for all in and out of the spotlight who are struggling with temptation. Pray for all who have been hurt by the unfaithfulness of a loved one. Finally, pray for those who live with the guilt of infidelity.

PARENTAL LOVE

I still cry when I see a newborn baby being rushed off
    to special care. Lord knows it still cuts right to the
    core when I think of my own son, my firstborn being
    whisked away from the Maternity Unit to the Children's
    Hospital.
That was back when I wasn't quite sure of you God. An
    angry agnostic I suppose you might say.
But as the ambulance doors closed I couldn't believe that
    something so tiny – just two days old – could come
    from nothing. The chips were down and the prognosis
    was not good. But that was the moment that I started to
    believe in you once again.
Now, I am nearing retirement and father of six happy,
    healthy children, every one of them, a gift from you
    O God, every single one just as precious as the first who
    nearly died.
I have given my life to you God in constant service and I
    always will, for that gift of parental love is something
    that you revealed to me in ways I could not imagine.
Like any parent, I have made my mistakes, plenty and
    some have cut deeper than others, but if I could just
    live out the way you love us as a parent, for one more
    day, I will.
You sent your only-begotten son to suffer for us and I
    know how gut-wrenching that might have been, for as
    a parent I know I would do anything to relieve a child's
    suffering.
Let my prayer be for parental love, wherever it might be.

Bless the parents who struggle to hold on to life itself.
Bless the parent who counts the money down the back of
    the sofa to make ends meet.
Bless the parents whose children are spread far across this
    world, torn by distance, not love.
Bless the parent who sits up all night checking for signs of
    infection.
Bless the parents whose children are truly carefree.
Bless the parent who stands proud at graduation.

Bless the parents whose love has been torn apart by
    bitterness and anger.
Bless the parents who barely notice their child.
Bless the parent who savours every moment.
Bless the parents who skype their grandchildren three
    thousand miles away.
Bless the parent who never had a role model on which to
    begin parenting.
Bless the parents whose parenting starts today cradling
    pounds and ounces of their own love.
And bless the parents who are only able to cradle the ashes
    of loss and bereavement.

Suggested Prayer Activity

Not all of us are blessed with being parents, or having parents to cherish, and sometimes that absence of either never being able to be a parent, or not knowing and loving our own parents can scar deep in peoples' lives. This prayer activity is offered with the deepest sensitivity intended:

Think of all the parents whom you have encountered recently. Friends, your own parents, your children as parents, bereaved parents, maybe even celebrity parents.

What is it about them that makes them special? What are the moments that you treasure the most. Do you have images or memories? Do you have photographs, certificates or memory boxes? Would you like to bring them out? If so, then take time to recollect, knowing that every memory is a prayer heard by God.

SACRIFICIAL LOVE

It takes a broken body
for humanity to recognise
the depth of unconditional love.
It takes a torn curtain
to sense the pain
of the relationships
shattered by abuse and denial.
It takes the silence of a day
to hear the weeping
of a world waiting to be embraced.
It takes the dawning of a new day
and the impossibility of an empty tomb,
for the possibility of longed-for love
to be shared.

Lord of love,
who turned His cheek
to accept the punishment
of those who feared the power
of God's love,
in the love we seek to offer
in Your name
make us daring and brave.

Where we have defined love
by the ability to be loved by others,
draw us back to Your definition.

Encourage us to hear the words
that ask us to love the unlovable.
In the empty places of our lives
may we welcome
the discomfort
of struggling to live
with opposite opinions.

In the breaking of bread
may the boundaries

of the familiar
be expanded
to encounter You
in the blessing of
hurts and anger laid low.   AMEN.

Suggested Prayer Activity

Read John 3:16–21

This passage is often linked to thinking about those who serve in the Armed Forces and around the time of Remembrance. Spend a little time focusing on those who serve in our Armed Forces.

Remember the task they face in areas of conflict as they negotiate with those they must work with and support each other in difficult situations.

Remember the family sacrifices they make, sometimes missing out on family celebrations and achievements as they carry out their duties … think about their families, who also make sacrifices as they try to carry on normal lives, while missing and worrying about a loved one.

There are others in our communities who make sacrifices because of their love. Spend some time thinking about those who care for a loved one who needs support in their living. Remember those who share their lives with those with mental health issues and limiting physical abilities. At times when there is no support, what is the isolation that is experienced? Some carers are young people caring for parents. What activities do they miss? What experiences are they unable to share?

These organisations might offer insight for prayer and advice for support:

http://www.carersuk.org/support
http://www.youngcarers.net

BROTHERLY/SISTERLY LOVE

Who is my sister and who is my brother?
You asked that question, Lord.
And Your answer didn't do much
for family relationships.

You, Lord, knew the special bond
that strings together not just siblings.
So while Your own stayed close by
You made brother and sister
of stranger and friend.

We are blessed
with brothers and sisters to love, Lord,
just as You were.
Not all share our parents or our past.
Not all have memories which touch ours.
Not all may know us as we were.
But all share a closeness that comes
not through blood
but through a binding of minds
and an opening of hearts.

Lord, bless those we call brothers and sisters.
The people who stay close by
even when we distance ourselves
in our choice of words and actions.
Those who know us better
than we know ourselves;
who tell it like it is even when we don't like it.
Those with whom we choose connection
for they fit around us
like familiar, comfortable clothes.

And bless us, Lord, Your brothers and sisters,
Your family and Your friends.
Stay close by; bind us to You,
wrap us in Your comforting love
that we might know true connection
in our relationship with You.   AMEN.

Suggested Prayer Activity

Those of us who have siblings and other relatives know the joy and heartache of family relations. Those who do not may crave the closeness and sense of identity that being part of a family brings. Jesus calls us all his brothers and sisters. Read Matthew 12:46–50 and reflect on who is your family.

Think about your close relatives, past and present and think about what connects you to them. Spend time praying for each one over the next few days and for any situations which may be difficult or joyful for them.

Think about distant relatives with whom you have not had contact for a long time and those who are estranged from the family circle. Try to find out more about them, either directly or through someone else. Pray for them and for what may be happening in their lives.

Think about your church family, those in your congregation and whom you meet through ecumenical events. Spend time each day praying for them and give thanks for the relationship you enjoy with them.

Think about good friends you consider as family and why you consider them brothers and sisters. Pray for them and give thanks for your friendship.

LOVE YOUR NEIGHBOUR

'Teacher, which is the greatest commandment in the Law?'
Jesus replied: '"Love the Lord your God with all your heart and with
all your soul and with all your mind." This is the first and greatest
commandment. And the second is like it: "Love your neighbour
as yourself." All the Law and the Prophets hang on these two
commandments.'

The second is like it.
The second is like it.

Loving God is like loving our neighbour.
Loving our neighbour is like loving God.

Do we avoid taking
our neighbour's name in vain?
Do we speak to our friends
of our neighbour's virtues?
Do we allow that sometimes,
as much as it pains us,
we do not have all the information
needed to understand the motives
and means of our neighbour?

Lord, my grandmother's words come to me,
it's no loss what a friend gets.
You made the world our friend.
Every beggar on the street,
every sly woman at work,
every boasting man on the bus,
every talent show contestant
every slum dweller
every drunk street stander
every benefits needer
every minister or elder
every every everyone.
They are our friends,
what they get IS what we get,
we and they, they and we, are the

same
thing:
Yours.

The second is like it.
The second is like it.

Suggested Prayer Activity

> *Without turning to Scripture, reflect on the story of the Good Samaritan.*
>
> What phrases and images spring to mind?
>
> *Now read or listen to Luke 10:25–42.*
>
> Were there any details you had forgotten or confused?
>
> What people or groups of people can you think of today who are lying beaten up, literally or metaphorically, at the wayside? Pray for them. Have you ever been a good Samaritan to someone?
>
> Who have been good neighbours and good Samaritans in your own life?
>
> Give thanks for them.
>
> Pray for the work of the voluntary organisation 'The Samaritans' who listen to and give advice on the problems of 'neighbours' through the medium of the phone.
>
> You may wish to read more on their website:
> www.samaritans.org
>
> Pray for all your immediate neighbours – those you know and those you don't.
>
> Pray for the community in which you live.
>
> Pray for those who have recently moved in,
>
> for single parents,
>
> for those who live alone
>
> and for families coping with relational or social problems.

LOVE OF ENEMY

You weren't short of enemies, Lord.
From the moment You were born
they were after Your blood.
You made kings resentful,
left lawmakers outraged,
offended your family
and upset the status quo.
Yet You still managed to love
those who angered and disturbed You,
those who labelled You
unlikeable and unreasonable.

Lord, I want to love as You did.
But I find my fondness
stretches as far as only my friends.
I want to care as You did.
But it seems my compassion
lasts as long as only I see fit.
I want to serve as You did.
But instead I save my energy
for those only I deem deserving.

I am not short of enemies, Lord,
those who question the choices
which make me who and what I am,
those whose creed and culture,
politics and lifestyle, status and standpoint
make it impossible for me to call them friends.
Help me to pray for them
not that they might change for my sake
but that I might love them for Your sake.
Help me to pray for them
not that they will become my friends
but that they remain Your friends.
Help me to pray for them
that I might find enough of Your
left over love to share.

And help me to pray for myself, Lord,
for I too am someone's enemy.
May they find it in their hearts
to love me a little too.   AMEN.

Suggested Prayer Activity

Jesus tells us to love our enemies. We all know how hard that is, for every day we encounter people for whom we find it difficult to have compassion and understanding. There are also people who consider us difficult to love, for they look upon us as their enemy.

Read Matthew 5:43–48 and make two lists – one of people you consider your enemies and the other of people who may consider you an enemy. Each day, pick a name from both lists and ask what it is that makes you enemies of one another. Ask yourself if there are ways in which you might be more accepting of who they are and what, if anything, you might do to change their perception of you.

Pray for understanding and tolerance. Pray for the strength to make changes and to have the courage of your convictions.

OLDER LOVE

Dear God,
I love seeing Love
walk hand in hand along the road –
an elderly couple in the default position
of their courting days.
Their love seems to fit like an old slipper
still comfortable and soft,
but with little holes
that have become part
of their growing wholeness.

I love seeing Love
struggling on and off buses –
two old companions winning the good fight
for their weekly coffee in town.
Their friendship warm like a hot water bottle,
still held reassuringly close,
mutual support and love based
on shared experiences
and treasured memories of good old days.

I love seeing Love
in the tender ministrations to an ageing person
from devoted child or carer to one
who knows the glorious sacrifice of parenthood.
Their love seems to uphold like support stockings
keeping the blood of life flowing
enabling tiny freedoms
and breaking up the clots of inactivity.

I love seeing Love
in the papery skinned hands
tremblingly breaking bread to share,
and holding, for dear life, on to the cup
that has sealed a lifetime relationship.
I sense the beat of the faithful old Bethlehem heart
and notice the arms though weakened with age
but still strong enough to cradle the weak.

Dear God,
I love seeing, what I think is Love,
between, to and from our senior citizens.
But I hate not discerning love,
in the lives of hidden older ones
seemingly cast adrift –
lover-less, childless, friendless, or faithless.
Dear God,
Help us to ensure that all our older ones know love. AMEN.

Suggested Prayer Activity

Abraham and Sarah had love into ripe old age.
Read their story over this month (*Genesis 18:1–15 and 21:1–8*).
Pray for all older couples still living together or apart because one is in care.

Jacob was old when his family finally reunited.
Read his story over this month (*Genesis 46*).
Can you think of older parents who long for reconciliation in the family?
Pray for older parents who still worry about their children.

Simeon and Anna were old when Jesus was presented in the temple.
Read their story this month (*Luke 2:22–38*).
Can you think of older people waiting for a special event?
Can you think of older people whose loving faith inspires you?
Pray for all older people in the church and in your community, especially the lonely.

Why not find out how you could bring love into the lives of older people.

Find out what opportunities there are in your own church and community for volunteering.

LOVE OF COUNTRY

Lord of an ancient nation,
my heart sings to You
with the pride I feel for my country.
So I give thanks for the history of my home.
For the rich and poor, wealthy and lowly
who have placed the common good of all people
at the heart of building a nation's confidence.
May my pride not blind me
to the strength of Your love
that builds relationships with neighbours.

Lord of an historic nation,
my eyes marvel at the creativity
of those who have designed and formed
the castles and kirks, the houses and tower-blocks.
Within each residence and work-place
may those who live, work and play
enjoy the opportunity of life in all its fullness.

Lord of a musical nation,
my ears have been filled
with the sounds of praise and lament.
May we always delight in those
who offer us a different perspective.
As the artist uses colour, clay or craft
to offer awareness hidden subjects,
through their eyes lead us
to new understandings of our country.

Lord of a working nation,
my hands are ready
to be employed in what you might ask of me this day.
In times of economic hardship
may I not lose sight of the bigger picture.
When my cup overflows, encourage me in generosity.
May the serving of Your kingdom
frame the ambitions and hopes
of all I love within this land.   AMEN.

Suggested Prayer Activity

How you might love your country.

Love your country as an active citizen: Proverbs 1:20–27
The passage speaks of Wisdom raising her voice in the streets, calling people to a different way to live. In loving our country there is an opportunity to take an active part in community living. How might we take part in the political process? To what current events could the voice of the Christian community bring a new view?

Love of your country with knowledge of history and stories: Exodus 12:14–20
Within the Gospels, we encounter Jesus' familiarity with his own religious and community tradition and story and he allows it to inform his encounters with others. The passage of the Exodus reminds us of Jesus eating with his disciples. How has our history shaped us? What are the positives and the negatives?

Love of your country through creativity and imagination: 1 Samuel 16:14–23
Our understanding of the variety of God's characters in greatly shaped by what we think are the writings of a simple Hebrew Shepherd, called David, who would become King. In the passage from Samuel we read that Saul's savage emotions were calmed by the creativity of David. Think about how national art and literature provoke a wealth of emotions within your own life.

Love of your country and its heroes: Acts 9:1–12
Throughout the Bible there are heroes of faith who inspire us to follow Christ. This passage offers two heroes, Paul at his conversion and Ananias who grasps courage to meet with a one-time persecutor of those who followed Jesus. Which of our country's heroes inspire us in our living? What are the qualities that we admire that could inform the faith we hope to show to the world?

THE LOVE OF GOD FOR US

Praise the Lord!
O give thanks to the Lord, for he is good;
for his steadfast love endures forever.

~ Psalm 106:1 ~

Prayer

I know You love me, Lord.

But what about that time when I closed
my eyes and ears to You,
when I turned away and chose to do what I knew
was not according to Your will?

And that time when I turned from You,
when I chose the way of least resistance,
avoiding the pitying looks of my peers
and their questioning of my intelligence?

And that time when I had to come to You,
disturbed and guilty,
distressed and full of shame,
for I had done wrong,
knowing full well that You would be displeased?

And that time when I had followed the crowd,
speaking their language,
using their words, vitriolic and cutting,
in the face of those not like us,
wounding them deeply
and doing them harm?

And that time when the lure of the darkness
pulled me in
and then I came to and remembered
that You are God,
that there is no other
and I felt like a worm on the ground
before You?

How can You love me, Lord?
How can You still love me?

How can I still love you?

My love for you is a thing of power,
made visible in the sacrifice
on the Cross.

My love has
the power to save, to heal,
to forgive;
the power to change you, to grow you,
to help you see;
the power to hold you, to cherish,
to care.

Come to Me, trusting in My love;
come to Me
for I love you with
all My heart, My mind,
My strength.

Come to Me
and rest.

> *Blessed be the Lord, the God of Israel,*
> *from everlasting to everlasting.*
> *And let all the people say, 'AMEN'.*
> *Praise the Lord!*
>
> ~ Psalm 106:48 ~

Suggested Prayer Activity

Collect pebbles as symbols of the burdens on your
heart. Find a space to lay them down and as you
contemplate the power of God's love to bring about
change in us, draw on each pebble a symbol of love
and forgiveness. You may want to place the pebbles
at the foot of a cross.

REMEMBERED LOVE

Why do we do it?
Why do we put love into the past tense?
Add a 'd' for death?

How often I have stood
at funerals or memorial services
and listened to the words,
'We pray for those who loved him most.'
Were those words true how easy it would be!
Here today – I love you.
Gone tomorrow – my love for you is past.

No! No! No!
I am still loving.
With the whole of my broken heart
I am still loving!
And even should I find new loves in my life
my old loves do not die.
It is not death that destroys love.
It is life's happenings and our responses
that can destroy love between humans.

And why do we say it?
'We will re-member them.'
We cannot put them back together.
We can recall, honour and pray for –
nothing more.

I have not done military service.
Yet I wear the loves who have gone before me
like medals shining in the light of the Son.

And when I take the bread and wine
and I hear You say, Lord,
'Do this to re-member me',
I think of your body on earth
in communion
with Your body in heaven.

Then in faith and hope and love,
abiding in these three,
I eat and drink
with my loves here
and my loves with You.

Nothing in life or in death,
can ever separate us
from Your love.

Lord, bless all who love.

Suggested Prayer Activity

In the Bible, the command to remember is an act
of love. The people of Israel are told to bind on
their foreheads or doorposts the words of the first
commandment 'You shall love the Lord your God,
with all your heart, and with all your soul, and with
all your might' (*Deuteronomy 6:4–9*).

The Israelites are also asked to remember the
covenant of loving relationship and promise
established between God and their ancestor,
Abraham. They are also told to 'love their
neighbours'. The commandments to love God and
neighbour are repeated by Jesus (*Luke 10:25–37*).

When we celebrate the sacrament of communion or
the Eucharist or Mass we act out the remembering
of God's love for us through the Cross of Christ. We
remember Jesus' commandment to love another as
He loved us (*John 13:34*).

You might like to reflect on how daily, you
remember God's love for you.

NEW LOVE

We thank you for the excitement of love at first sight.
We treasure the new reasons to love that are revealed daily.
We trust in your grace and forgiveness
that offer us the chance to begin again.
We love the excitement, tension and drama
that is simply God-given in new love.

And it's Yours God.
We know that new love begins in You
for you have told and shown us
through the innocence and naiveté of Adam and Eve,
the vulnerability and risk of the young couple, Mary and
        Joseph,
the hand-in-glove fit of Priscilla and Aquila,
The comical timing of Abraham and Sarah
the irreconcilable differences of Samson and Delilah
and the unwavering devotion of Jacob for Rachel.

You bless new love, God, in all its myriad forms:
excitement
new experiences
kindred spirit
deep conversation from sunset to dawn
and the goose bumps of new, expectant love.

You also bring new love when love is worn out:
broken
desperate, or simply vanished.
You show us how to begin again
and your forgiveness and grace teaches us
to find love anew.

You share new love in Jesus Christ
whose love was no stranger to controversy:
direct and Uncompromising
love that kept no boundaries
and a love that led to the cross
and the new love of resurrection.

May we cherish and treasure new love
in the transforming name of our Lord Jesus
and the love that is made new by Christ.

Lord Jesus Christ you make all things new:
do the same with love
do the same with love
do the same with love.   AMEN.

Suggested Prayer Activity

Pray for the people and the places where you would
hope that God could bring new love.

Reflect too on the renewal of love in your own life.

Appendix

Using *Pray Now* as a worship resource

Below is an example of how to take a day of *Pray Now* and augment it to produce a shorter act of communal worship. Essentially all the sections can be used or just the leader's introduction followed by the Bible Reading, the Meditation, a short silence, the Prayer and the Blessing – this may be all that is required for opening devotions.

The service may be led by one voice but has opportunity for several voices. Although the sections are read, the group may appreciate having individual copies of 'Revealing Love' to use during the service or to take away with them.

Bearing All Things (Day 20)

(*You may wish to have music playing or a candle burning to create a worshipful atmosphere. Also, you may wish to incorporate some symbolic act in which each person is given a stone at the beginning and invited to think of their stone as a particular burden or burdens that they leave at the foot of a cross at the end of the service.*)

Leader   In our worship we are invited to reflect on how we cope with all the things we have to bear. We begin by listening to a reading from St Paul's letter to the Galatian Church. Galatia was a Roman province which is now part of modern day Turkey. Paul was encouraging the believers to help one another stay faithful and carry each others' burdens.

Reading   Galatians 6:1–5

Song	'Brother, sister, let me serve you' (*CH4 694 music and words by Richard A. M. Gillard, arranged by Betty Jane Pulkingham*) *Or* 'What a friend we have in Jesus' (*CH4 547 music by Charles Crozat Converse and words by Joseph Scriven*)
Leader	*'Bear one another's burdens and in this way you will fulfil the law of Christ.'* 'The Law of Christ' is an expression used by St Paul. What do you think it means? Is Paul thinking of Jesus' seminal commandment: 'Love one another, as I have loved you'? (*John 13:34*) Listen now to this short meditation. There will be a short silence afterwards for our own thoughts.
Meditation	I cannot bear all things. I have tried and I have failed. But you, St Paul have shown me the error of my ways. It is Love that can bear all things. Even You, Christ, did not bear all things alone. You needed the love of family, friends and disciples. And when it was too much to bear in Gethsemane, on Golgotha, carrying the weight of the world on Your shoulders God's love carried You, His precious Son.

It is Love alone
that can bear all things

Yet we cannot love alone.
For love is relationship,
is giving and receiving.

So help me share
in bearing all things Lord,
joining heart and hands with others
to carry life itself.

Silence *(optional)*

Reflection *(optional)*

Leader What came out of that meditation for you?
     Does anyone want to share their thoughts?

     Or

     Have you ever felt that you are carrying the
     weight of the world on your shoulders?

     Is there someone to whom you have off-loaded?

     Do you think the expression 'a load shared, is
     a load halved' is true?

     What part has prayer played in your life when
     you have felt heavy burdened?

     Are you a way of helping to carry someone
     else's burden just now?

     What does the apparently random selection of
     Simon of Cyrene to carry the Cross of Jesus say
     to you? (Luke 23:26)

     (you will wish to select a few questions)

Prayer Loving Lord,
     may all who can no longer endure
     their responsibilities
     or their circumstances
     hear Jesus' say:
     'Come to me all you that are weary
     and carrying heavy burdens':

Those who feel the weight of illness
or the weight of care for one who is ill;

Those who feel the pressure of work
or the pressure of no work:

Those who bear the millstone of grief
or the millstone of guilt;

Those who suffer daily persecution
or daily abuse;

Those who carry hunger in their bodies
or hunger in their souls;

Those individuals or groups
whom we name before You now

* * *

*(There is a place here for additional extempore
prayers of intercession)*

'Come to me,
and I will give you rest.'

Lord,
when we ourselves
are tested beyond our means,
give us the humble faith
to come to You
but also to recognise
that Your help
still comes in human form.
Amen.

Blessing   *(This may be spoken by the leader, or another,
or said together or sung together.)*

May Christ's yoke fit easily upon you.
May His burden be ever light.
May His love gentle your heart.
And may you be blessed
by the One who endures all things.
Amen.

Additional Resources

Other relevant hymns:

'Lord, can this really be' (CH4 205)
'Rejoice in God's saints' (CH4 742)
'Take up your cross', the Saviour said' (CH4 402)
'What a friend we have in Jesus' (CH4 547)

Acknowledgements

Pray Now 'Revealing Love' was prepared by members of the *Pray Now* Group: Adam Dillon, Graham Fender-Allison, Carol Ford, Mark Foster, Tina Kemp, Ishbel McFarlane, MaryAnn Rennie and Peggy Roberts.

Daily headline Scripture quotations are taken from the *New Revised Standard Version*, © 1989 Division of Christian Education of the National Council of Churches of Christ in the United States of America, published by Oxford University Press.

Day 23 Blessing printed with permission – Copyright © George F. MacLeod, 1985, *The Whole Earth Shall Cry Glory*, Wild Goose Publications, Glasgow.

Extracts from Gerard Kelly, *Twitturgies* and *Prodigal Blessing* used by permission of River Publishing.

Graham would like to express his thanks to the Very Revd David Lunan and Maggie Lunan who first taught him how to pray.

Contact Us

For further information about *Revealing Love* and other material from the Mission and Discipleship Council's Faith Expressions Team, contact:

> FAITH EXPRESSION TEAM
> Mission and Discipleship Council
> Church of Scotland
> 121 George Street
> Edinburgh EH2 4YN
>
> Tel: 0131 225 5722
> Fax: 0131 220 3113
>
> e-mail: mand@cofscotland.org.uk

A range of Church of Scotland publications and stationery is available from Saint Andrew Press:

> www.standrewpress.com